Early 16th Century

Accounts of the Great Wall reach Europe via Europeans traveling to China. In the 19th century, firsthand accounts, travelogues, and illustrations help create fantastical myths about the wall's size—such as that it is visible from the moon!

1980s

China's leader Deng Xiaoping starts a campaign to repair and preserve the Great Wall as part of the nation's history. It is designated a UNESCO World Heritage site in 1987.

1424–1620

The Ming dynasty embarks on the biggest wall-building program in Chinese history. New walls and beacon towers are constructed, fortifications are restored and extended, and troops, firearms, and artillery are positioned along the lines.

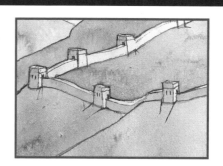

2006

The Chinese government introduces laws to preserve the Great Wall, parts of which have deteriorated badly through neglect.

Map of the Seven Warring States

When Ying Zheng (who later took the title Qin Shihuangdi) became ruler of the state of Qin in 247 B.C., at the age of thirteen, he worked to unify the whole of China by conquering the other six of the Seven Warring States—the seven largest and strongest Chinese states during the period.

Zheng used a ruthless strategy of assassinating rival leaders and defeating their armies in battle. Qin's most formidable opponent was the state of Chu. Although the Chu forces were initially able to repel the invading Qin army, by 224 B.C. the Chu side had suffered a catastrophic military defeat and their leader, Xiang Yan, was killed in action.

Ying Zheng was able to claim unchallenged control of China by 221 B.C.

Author:
Jacqueline Morley studied English at
Oxford University, England. She has taught
English and history, and now works as a freelance
writer. She has written historical fiction and
nonfiction for children.

Artist:
David Antram was born in Brighton, England,
in 1958. He studied at Eastbourne College of Art
and then worked in advertising for 15 years before
becoming a full-time artist. He has illustrated many
children's nonfiction books.

Series Creator:
David Salariya was born in Dundee, Scotland.
He has illustrated a wide range of books and has
created and designed many new series for
publishers both in the UK and overseas. In 1989,
he established The Salariya Book Company. He
lives in Brighton, England, with his wife, illustrator
Shirley Willis, and their son, Jonathan.

Editor: **Sophie Izod**

PAPER FROM
SUSTAINABLE
FORESTS

Published in Great Britain in 2017 by
The Salariya Book Company Ltd
25 Marlborough Place, Brighton BN1 1UB

ISBN-13: 978-0-531-23838-7 (lib. bdg.) 978-0-531-23160-9 (pbk.)

A CIP catalog record for this book is available
from the Library of Congress.

Printed and bound in China.
Printed on paper from sustainable sources.

1 2 3 4 5 6 7 8 9 10 R 26 25 24 23 22 21 20 19 18 17

You Wouldn't Want to Work on the Great Wall of China!

Written by
Jacqueline Morley

Illustrated by
David Antram

Created and designed by
David Salariya

Defenses You'd Rather Not Build

Franklin Watts®
An Imprint of Scholastic Inc.

Contents

Introduction

You're a poor farmer living in China around 215 B.C. With plenty of things to worry about— bad weather, poor crops, and big taxes to pay— you've barely noticed the political upheavals taking place around you recently. A few years ago, China as one nation did not exist. The land was divided between rival states who had been fighting each other for centuries. But now a really strong ruler from the state of Qin has emerged. He has united the country and called himself Qin Shihuangdi, which means "First Great Emperor of China." He is ruthless and cruel. No one dares to disobey his orders and he does not care how many people die carrying them out. You are one of the unlucky thousands he sends to build a huge defensive wall 1,800 miles long on China's northern border. It's known as the Great Wall of China and it's still there today.

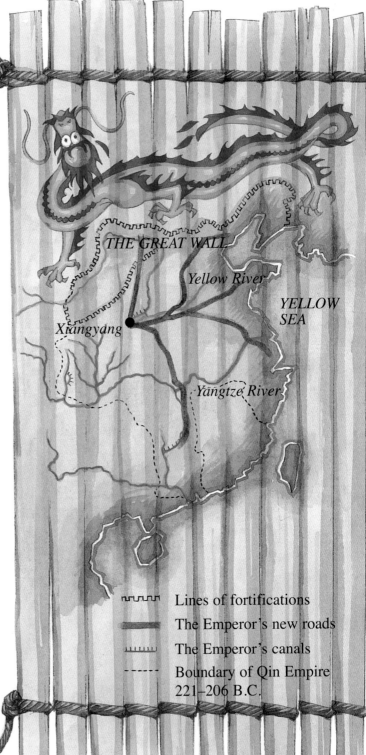

THE GREAT WALL

Yellow River

YELLOW SEA

Xiangyang

Yangtze River

ᴖᴖᴖ Lines of fortifications

━━━ The Emperor's new roads

ᴗᴗᴗᴗ The Emperor's canals

- - - - Boundary of Qin Empire 221–206 B.C.

The First Great Emperor

The Emperor has "all-seeing eyes, the nose of a hornet, the voice of a jackal, and the heart of a wolf." That's how one of his advisors described him (before fleeing for his life). You saw the Emperor once, and it's a fair description. He was driving along one of the many new highways he ordered built to speed communications and tighten his control. He has made everyone use the same currency, writing style, weights and measures, and distance between their cart wheels (so they can run in the same ruts). There are rules for everything.

How He Rules:

HE'S BUILT a magnificent new capital, Xiangyang, and made the headstrong nobles hand in their swords, leave their lands, and live there under his watchful eye.

THROUGHOUT the land, government officials write him reports on strips of bamboo laced together and rolled up—there is no paper.

THE EMPEROR is a tireless worker. He weighs his pile of reports to make sure he's done his daily quota.

DISOBEYING him is most unwise. Punishments include beheading, being buried alive, and being cut in half at the waist.

Handy Hint

Don't criticize the Emperor or you will never be promoted—if you survive at all!

Everlasting Rule

Build, build, build!

POOR PEOPLE everywhere are forced to work on the Emperor's projects—soldiers, convicts, slaves, and ordinary people just like you. You see large numbers of them being marched off to dig canals or to build new roads and fortifications. Your time will come.

The Emperor is very superstitious and terrified of dying. He hopes to cheat death by finding the "elixir of life," a magic substance that will make him immortal. He has sent expeditions far and wide to seek it, so far with no success. If this plan fails, he has another one. He has 700,000 workers building a tomb containing a model of his kingdom, so that he will continue ruling in the next world. They are also making an army to guard it—over 8,000 life-sized figures of men, horses, and chariots made from terra-cotta and buried underground.

UNDERGROUND TOMB: In the inner chamber of the Emperor's tomb, a dragon ferries his copper coffin across a model of his kingdom complete with gem-studded palaces and towers. The ceiling represents the star-filled sky, while below, the rivers of China, made in quicksilver, flow into a quicksilver ocean. (As described by a Chinese historian of c.100 B.C. It has not been excavated.)

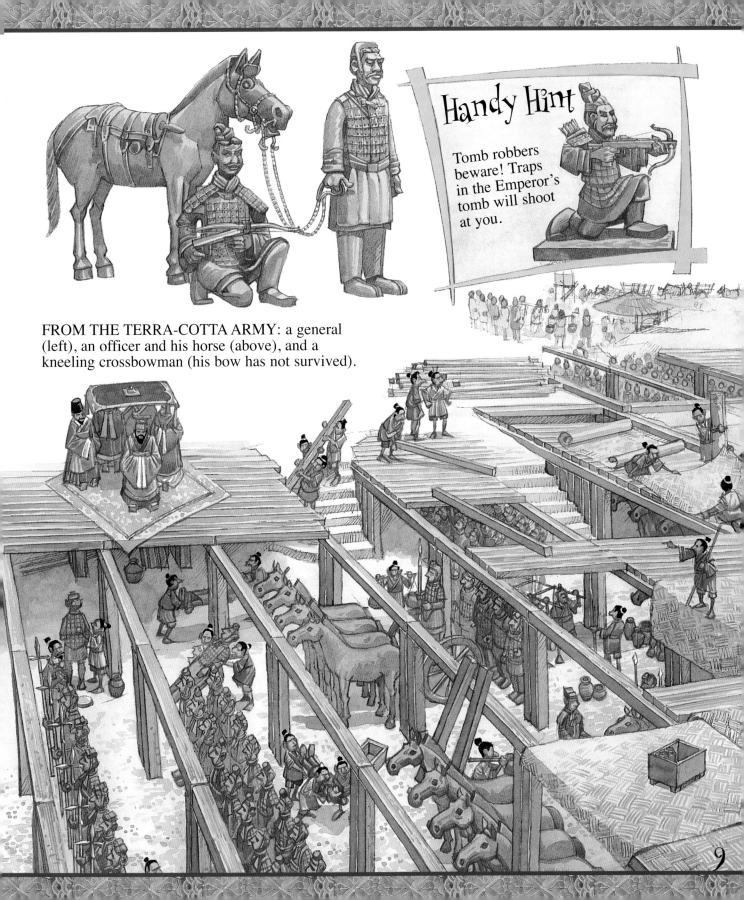

Handy Hint

Tomb robbers beware! Traps in the Emperor's tomb will shoot at you.

FROM THE TERRA-COTTA ARMY: a general (left), an officer and his horse (above), and a kneeling crossbowman (his bow has not survived).

A Hard Life

DROUGHT AND FLOOD: Bad weather can ruin all your hopes. If no rain falls, your crops will shrivel. If it does fall, the Yellow River may flood and drown them.

Like most of the Emperor's subjects, you live in the country and scrape a living from a small piece of land. It belongs to your father, who's getting old now but still makes all the decisions, and you must obey him. That is the duty of Chinese sons and daughters, no matter how old they are. You work every day of the year, but still it's hard to grow enough to feed the family—you, your parents, and your sister—and to have anything left over to sell. Every year you pay tax to the Emperor, and this is calculated according to the size of your land, not the size of your crop. When the harvest is poor, there's nothing left once the tax has been paid. In order to eat and to buy seed for next year's crop you have to borrow money, and once you get into debt it is very hard to get out. Many poor farmers are ruined this way.

From Bad to Worse:

A You borrow money from a rich landowner to pay your debts.

B You have to sell animals and tools to pay him back.

C You can't work the farm without your tools so you are forced to sell it to the landowner. You become his tenant and do all the work, and he keeps all the profit.

D The last straw: a conscription officer selects you to do forced labor.

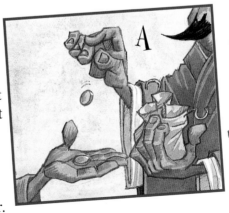

Handy Hint

If you're desperately in debt, sell your children (daughters first) as slaves.

The Burning of the Books

Some scholars who study the writings of past thinkers have been brave enough to criticize the Emperor. They say he cannot rule exactly as he pleases, for books of wisdom explain that a ruler has duties towards his subjects as well as powers over them. The Emperor intends to stop this dangerous talk. He has ordered all books (except those on farming, medicine, and soothsaying) to be handed in and burned on public bonfires. Anyone quoting books to criticize the Emperor will be put to death. Already over 460 leading scholars have been buried alive.

SEARCHING: Soldiers are searching houses and gardens for hidden books. If they find any, the owner is executed on the spot.

BURYING BOOKS: A terrified old scholar begs you to hide a box of his precious books by burying them in your field. He pays you well.

Handy Hint

To preserve a well-loved book, learn it by heart.

CAUGHT! "I only did it for the money!" you plead when you are caught. You're sentenced to five years on the Great Wall.

BACK IN THE CELLS, you ask what the Great Wall is. "They call it the longest graveyard in the world," a fellow prisoner tells you.

Raiders from the North

You're going to China's northern border, where people live in terror of the Xiongnu, the wandering herdsmen from the plains. Their animals provide their food, clothes, and shelter, but for other needs they go trading—or raiding! They are incredibly skilled horsemen, swooping out of nowhere, killing villagers and taking whatever they want. The Emperor has decided to build a huge wall to keep them out. It will run the length of his kingdom from east to west, linking some existing walls and going far beyond them. He wants it built fast, and he doesn't care how many people die building it.

What You've Heard About the Xiongnu:

HOUSING: They don't live in houses like normal people but in round tents made of animal skins. Even their clothes are made from skin instead of cloth.

FOOD AND DRINK: They eat and drink the most disgusting things. For instance, they drink milk and make cheese, which no Chinese person would dream of doing.

NO TASTE: When Chinese diplomats brought them expensive gifts, they turned their noses up at the most delicious delicacies.

Attack!

Handy Hint

Watch out at harvest time. While everyone is in the fields, the Xiongnu will raid the village.

NO STYLE: They say silk trousers wear out if you ride in them for a week.

The Journey North

Branded, put in a convict's rough hemp robe, and chained to the next man, you're being marched to the Wall. From your home village in central China, this means a six-to-eight-week journey on foot. As you go further north, more and more lines of convicts pour in from side roads, until the route is almost blocked with them. You have no idea where you are, you just stumble on exhausted. The guards don't care what state you're in as long as they get you to the Wall on time. Several people have collapsed and died.

The 6-8 Week Journey:

IN MANY PARTS the roads are terrible. You must clamber up slopes and wade through rivers with no bridges.

CROSSING DENSE forest is the worst, for it's well-known that demons live there. You are terrified.

Handy Hint

Cheer up. At least you're not being executed like an official you pass on the road.

SOMETIMES the road is just a wooden walkway, clinging to the side of a gorge.

THE LAST STRETCH crosses harsh desert.

FINALLY you arrive at a military encampment by the Wall.

Walk faster!

The Emperor's Great Wall

WEAK POINTS in the wall, where rivers cross it, are guarded by especially large towers full of soldiers.

SMALLER TOWERS are put close together so that raiders storming the Wall are never out of arrow range.

Your first thought on seeing the Wall is, "A wall can't be that long!" And this is just the part they've built so far—miles of it, twisting and turning like a wriggling dragon along the highest ridges of ground. It's guarding China from the wilderness beyond, where lawless people and cruel demons live. The towers are set at regular intervals along the Wall and manned by soldiers constantly on guard. General Meng T'ien, who is in charge of this great project, has put 300,000 troops to work on the Wall and, just as importantly, on the roads to protect the supplies. You soon learn to watch for the arrival of the grain wagons. If they've had an accident or if their contents get stolen on the way here, you'll soon be starving.

THE WALL'S AMAZING number of towers is explained very differently by ordinary people. They say that the First Great Emperor galloped the whole length of the Wall on his magic flying horse, and wherever its hooves touched the Wall a tower sprang up.

Building the Wall

Under the whip, day in, day out, your work is endless, and no one cares if you are sick or dead. You build the Wall over mountains and across desert. In rocky areas you use stone, but in most places there isn't any suitable stone and the whole wall has to be made of pounded dirt. When you're in one of the supply gangs, you dig dirt or carry it to the site and tip it into a wooden frame. If you're in a frame gang you spread the dirt out thinly, no more than 5 inches deep, and ram it down with pounders. When that layer is hard and dry, a new one goes on top. When the stack is high enough, the frame is taken down and set up in the next spot. It takes much sweat and many days to build a section 33 feet tall and wide enough for five horsemen to ride side-by-side along its top.

SOAKED TO THE SKIN: Weather never makes the work stop. You carry loads, haul logs, and pound dirt in pouring rain.

SWELTERING HEAT: In blazing summer heat you hack through undergrowth to make a clearing for a new stretch of the Wall.

FREEZING COLD: Chilled to the bone in icy mountains, you cut through solid rock to make a level foundation for the Wall.

Handy Hint

Don't dig graves for workers who die. Pour the bodies into the foundations and they will soon be buried.

WATCH YOUR STEP: No one cares about your safety. You stagger under heavy loads all day, often up dangerous slopes...

AN EMPTY STOMACH: Only boiled mush again for supper! The army is growing food locally now, but there is not always enough.

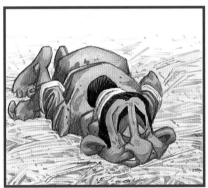

ALL IN A DAY'S WORK: After working every hour of daylight, you fall asleep exhausted on your patch of straw, inside a crowded tent.

Along the Watch Tower

After three years of hard labor, your sentence has been lightened to military service and you're stationed on a watch tower along the Wall you helped build! Army life is tough with cramped quarters, iron discipline, and constant inspections by the company commander. If anything moves out on the dusty plain, it means danger. Immediately you light a beacon fire—one column of smoke (or flame by night) for up to 500 raiders sighted, two for up to 3,000 and three for more than that. From beacon to beacon, the signal passes swiftly to the next garrison to summon help.

ABSOLUTE OBEDIENCE: An officer who killed two of the enemy without waiting for orders was executed for disobedience.

Handy Hint

Burning wolf dung makes the clearest signal. It makes black smoke that is easy to spot.

GATHERING TIMBER from beyond the Wall is a scary job, but the tower must never run out.

SWEEP THE SAND: Outside the Wall the sandy soil is swept smooth so that enemy footprints will show up.

A HORRIBLE "DRY FOG" DAY: Wind fills the air with fine sand, which blots out all the light from the sun. This makes it hard to see.

WINTERS on the Wall are no joke. The snow and wind make sentry duty miserable.

25

Guarding a Gate

Day to Day:

POSTAL SERVICE: You take letters to the next postal station along the Wall.

You've been transferred to a large garrison that guards a gate. It's the military headquarters for this stretch of the Wall, and its general has 100,000 men under his command. There has to be a gate in the Wall wherever it crosses a route used by traveling merchants from either side of the border. This means that when you're on gate duty it's your job to police it. You check passports, search wagons for goods being smuggled in, and watch out for illegal immigrants and criminals on the run.

GOTCHA! You've caught an army deserter (left) who was trying to slip through the gate.

CHECKING WAGONS (above left): He says it's only firewood underneath that cover, but is it?

MENDING THE WALL: Your section includes some older wall that's starting to crumble.

ALARM! Raiders have been sighted! You all grab weapons and rush into line.

INSPECTION: You dread the general spotting something about you that's not perfect.

A Lifetime by the Wall

Time passes. You hear that the Emperor has died. After a violent revolution, a former rebel is now Emperor. But all this matters little to you.

You've finished your army service but you're stranded here, without the money or the permit to make the long journey home. Your father is dead, your farm is sold, and your sister is married and part of another family. There's no choice but to make your home here in northernmost China, with its hot summers, freezing winters, and hard, dry soil. It's government policy to settle people here to protect the border and to grow food for the army. You've been granted land, you've married a local girl, and you're farming again—but you're facing a lifetime by the Wall.

"FIND ME THE ISLAND of the Immortals," the Emperor ordered, desperate to escape death. But his efforts are in vain.

HE DIED unexpectedly on a tour of eastern China. Plotting to seize power, the ministers with him tried to conceal his death. The Emperor traveled in a covered chariot, but his body started to smell. To hide this, they put a cart of rotting fish behind the chariot.

28

Handy Hint

If the Emperor sends you on an impossible mission, it's best not to return.

HEARING THE Emperor was dead, his long-oppressed people started a revolt, led by a laborer facing execution.

THE REBELS TAKE OVER: The capital burned for three months, and soon after the entire Qin family were dead.

Index

Did You Know?

The Great Wall of China has fascinated outsiders for many hundreds of years. Early descriptions of the fortifications by Arab travelers and writers like Rashid-al-Din Hamadani were often confused with the mythical walls of steel supposedly built by Alexander the Great.

European descriptions of the wall began in the early 1600s. One of the earliest eyewitness accounts was from Ivan Petlin, a Siberian Cossack who traveled to China in 1619 on a mission for the Russian embassy. Although these descriptions were initially quite accurate, as the Ming dynasty continued to extend the wall, Western stories about it became more embellished and fantastical.

The extraordinary stories of travelers and missionaries eventually gave rise to the Orientalism of the 18th century, a time when Europeans saw China as a magical realm that was both spectacular and frightening due to its impressive size. Voltaire, the French philosopher and writer, shared this viewpoint, admiring the Great Wall but also calling it a "monument to fear."

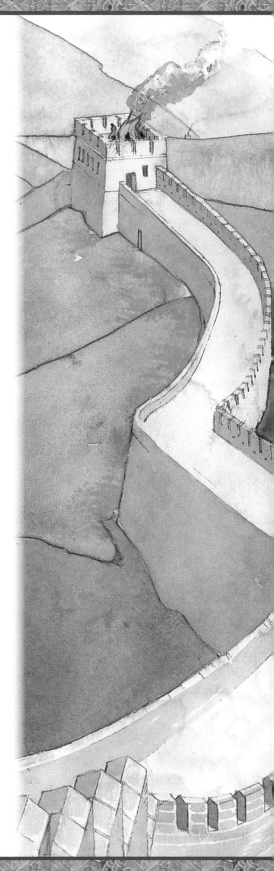

Top Wonders of the Ancient World

The Hanging Gardens of Babylon

Traditionally, the Hanging Gardens are said to have been built in the ancient city of Babylon by King Nebuchadnezzar II in 600 B.C. The structure was a series of tiered platforms, each housing a spectacular garden filled with plants and trees of all kinds. However, due to the lack of solid evidence, many have concluded that the gardens are only a myth and never really existed.

Statue of Zeus at Olympia

Created by the Greek sculptor Phidias around 435 B.C., this was a giant statue representing the god Zeus sitting on a wooden throne studded with gold and precious stones. It was erected in the Temple of Zeus in Olympia, but was destroyed in the 5th century A.D. The only knowledge we have of what it looked like comes from ancient Greek descriptions and images on ancient coins.

The Colossus of Rhodes

This statue of the Greek god of the Sun, Helios, was referred to as one of the Seven Wonders of the Ancient World. Erected on the Greek island of Rhodes, it stood nearly 110 feet (33.5 meters) tall and was made from iron and bronze. Sadly, it was badly damaged in an earthquake in 226 B.C. and the remains were never restored, so it was eventually melted down and the metal sold.

Statue of Zeus